D1393695

# ANIMAL NAVIGATORS

*Jeremy Cherfas*

CASSELL

# Contents

Introduction 3

Chapter 1 Movement and Migration 4
Why migrate? 4
Learning about migration 5
The ancient world 6
Ringing birds 7
Studying bird movements 8

Chapter 2 Navigating in the Air:
Birds 10
How do birds navigate? 11
Homing pigeons 12
Learning and instinct 14

Chapter 3 Navigating in the Air:
Bees 16
Using the sun 16
How bees give directions 17
The dance of the bees 18
How did the code come into
being? 19

Chapter 4 Navigating in the Air:
Butterflies and Bats 20
Migrating bats 21

Chapter 5 Navigating on Land 22
Ant navigators 23
The migrating herds 24

Chapter 6 Navigating under Water 26
From ocean to river 27
From river to ocean 28
The biggest navigators 28

Chapter 7 People and Navigation 29

Astounding Facts 31
Glossary 31
Index 32
Further Reading and Study 32

**Note to the Reader**

In this book there are some words in the text which are printed in **bold** type. This shows that the word is listed in the Glossary on page 31. The glossary gives a brief explanation of important words which may be new to you.

**Cassell Publishers Limited**
Villiers House, 41/47 Strand,
London WC2N 5JE

© Text Jollands Editions 1991
© Illustrations Cassell Publishers Limited 1991

All rights reserved. No part of this publication may be reproduced or transmitted in any form or by any means, electronic or mechanical including photocopying, recording or any information storage or retrieval system, without prior permission in writing from the publishers.

First published 1991

**British Library Cataloguing in Publication Data**
Cherfas, Jeremy
Animal navigators. – (How animals behave)
I. Title   II. Series
591.51

ISBN 0–304–31975–9

Editorial planning by Jollands Editions
Designed by Alison Anholt-White

Typeset by Fakenham Photosetting Ltd
Colour origination by Golden Cup Printing Co., Ltd,
Hong Kong
Printed in Great Britain by Eagle Colourbooks Ltd.
Glasgow

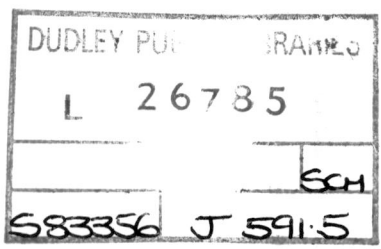

DUDLEY PUBLIC LIBRARIES

L 26785

583356   J 591·5

*Front Cover:* Long-eared bats in flight. These animal navigators are found in Europe and North America. (Photo by Kim Taylor, Bruce Coleman Ltd.)

*Back Cover:* The author (Photo by Rachel Pearcey)

# Introduction

Have you ever been lost? Really lost, so that you did not know which way to go? I have, in the middle of a strange city, with cars hooting around me as I struggled with a map. I had to find out where I was, where I wanted to be, and how to get there. In other words, I had to navigate.

Navigation is the science of finding your way about. It might be a short trip, finding your way home when you have just moved to a new school. Or it could be a longer journey, all the way from your home to the seaside or the mountains for a holiday. We use signposts and landmarks, maps and compasses, and even computers and other complicated equipment, to find our way about. Some animals are excellent navigators. This book is about how these animals and how some people navigate without maps, signposts or gadgets.

Some animals seem to have an inbuilt sense of direction. They know where to go without having to learn the direction. Others learn their way by trial and error. Some make regular long journeys, like the arctic tern, that flies almost all the way from the South Pole to the North Pole to breed. Others go on shorter journeys, like the limpet, that creeps from its shelter on a rock to feed a metre or so away. But they all need to navigate.

An Arctic tern in flight. These birds fly over 20,000 kilometres from the Antarctic to their Arctic breeding grounds. The bird's bill is normally black, but turns blood-red at breeding time.

A huge flock of migrating snow geese (white) and Canada geese (brown).

# Movement and Migration

Some scientists distinguish between migration and other kinds of movement. They say that migration is a long journey to and fro that is usually made regularly, every year for example. Swallows spend half the year breeding in Europe or North America, and migrate to Africa or South America, where they spend the second half of the year feeding.

Other movement, they say, is not always between such fixed places and does not happen so regularly. A water vole, which leaves the safety of its nest in a burrow and wanders about looking for food or a mate, travels along different paths and at different times before coming back to the burrow. It moves, but it does not migrate.

## Why migrate?

You may ask why an animal needs to migrate from one place to another. If an area is good, why not stay there? Because it may be good some of the time, but not at others. Many birds breed in one place and spend the rest of the year somewhere else. Usually, the breeding area has plenty of food, but only for a short while.

A bald eagle seen in Alaska with a migrating salmon which it has caught. This bird is the national symbol of the United States of America.

In the winter months the Arctic tundra freezes over and cannot support life. Caribou antlers can be seen in the foreground of the picture. These animals migrate southwards in herds as winter approaches. See also the photograph on page 23.

The frozen **tundra** is like that. Most of the year it is cold and barren, but in the spring it comes to life and there are dense swarms of insects. Countless flocks of birds arrive to breed, feeding on the small insects. Come the winter, however, and they have to find somewhere warmer with food, so off they fly.

## Learning about migration

Ancient peoples knew that animals came and went with the seasons. The American Indians of the Pacific coast of North America gathered by the rivers each spring to catch the salmon which were swimming upstream to mate. The brown bears and bald eagles would join them, all feasting on the migrating fish.

The American Indians made up myths and stories to explain nature's bounty. On the other side of the world, people noticed that animals vanished at some times of the year, and they too tried to explain it.

A brown bear in Alaska about to catch a leaping salmon as it migrates upstream to breed. Brown bears are found in northern Europe and in North America.

# The ancient world

Aristotle, the Greek scientist and philosopher, who lived between 384 and 322 BC, wrote about migration in one of his books. He knew that some animals went south in the winter, and returned in the spring. He noticed that in a migrating flock of pelicans, the birds take turns in being at the front. He also discovered that birds about to migrate grow fatter. The fat is an extra fuel supply. All that is true, but Aristotle made one mistake which was not corrected until the eighteenth century.

He thought that some birds, most notably swallows, did not migrate but simply hid themselves and **hibernated** through the winter. His proof was that in winter you could sometimes find birds 'asleep' in holes. In fact, they were probably dead. But the idea that swallows hibernated lasted a long time and some people even thought that they plunged into the water and buried themselves in the mud at the bottom of streams.

A flock of white pelicans seen over Israel, during their migration from northern Europe. These large birds fly in formation and fish together.

Swallows, found throughout the northern hemisphere, collect together in flocks as winter approaches. Then they migrate southwards to warmer places, such as Central America, North Africa and northern Australia.

Part of the problem was that travel was far harder for people than for swallows, so there was no way of following the birds and seeing for certain where they went. The breakthrough came when someone marked a bird by putting a ring around its leg.

## Ringing birds

One of the first rings we know about was worn by a swallow that nested in a château in France about 200 years ago. A nobleman, hiding after the French Revolution, put it on the bird. He discovered that the same bird returned to the same nest three years in a row. Of course, the ring did not tell the nobleman where the bird went when it was not at the castle.

Ringing birds is quite painless for the bird and the rings are so light that they do not interfere with flight. Ringing enables scientists to learn about the movements of birds and helps in their protection. On the left is a bird-ringing station in Israel. Radar is used to study bird migration.

In 1899, a scientist in Denmark made the first rings of **aluminium**. Rings like this are still used today. They are very light, and do not rust, so they last well. Each ring is stamped with a number and the address of the people who put it on. If you find a bird with a ring, you should send the details back. That way, we learn how long birds live, where they go, and how fast they can travel.

In Britain, about half a million birds are ringed each year. Birds ringed in Britain have appeared in Australia, South America, and even on the eastern coast of the USSR. And birds from almost every country that puts rings on them have turned up in Britain. Without these rings, we would know far less about bird migration.

## Studying bird movements

Ringing birds is one way of studying their movements, and there are similar tags for other kinds of animals, such as fish. There are many other techniques too. **Radar** operators, peering at their screens, often see flocks of birds passing high overhead. They can measure the speed and direction in which the birds are travelling, and sometimes identify the **species** and size of flock.

A gharial fitted with a radio transmitter. It is being released in Nepal by the late Sir Peter Scott who was a great animal lover. The gharial is a kind of crocodile that feeds mainly on fish which it catches in its slender snout.

Another method is to use an activity cage. This automatically records the direction an animal prefers. One of the simplest sorts is an inked pad, like the ones you use with a rubber stamp, at the bottom of a cone of paper. A bird that is migrating tries to climb out of the cone, leaving inky footprints that show the direction in which it wants to go. A more up-to-date version has many perches connected to a computer, which records which perch the bird likes to sit on.

Some scientists have followed birds and butterflies in an aeroplane. Others have used satellites high above the Earth to track the signals from a powerful radio transmitter attached to the animal. That way, they have mapped out the exact journeys of whales, seals, and even albatrosses and are finally beginning to understand how animals migrate. They know most about birds.

Above, radio-tracking condors in California, and, below, a Canada goose fitted with a lightweight radio transmitter.

The blackpoll warbler is a little bird that spends its summers in the USA and Canada. As winter approaches, the birds in New England go on a feeding binge, doubling their weight from 12 grams to 24 grams in just two weeks. The extra fat will power four or five days of non-stop flying. One evening, when there is wind from the north-west, the birds take off. They climb to about 1,000 metres and fly south-east, over the Atlantic, passing over Bermuda and the islands of the Caribbean. Finally they land in Brazil, 4,000 kilometres away. While New England is blanketed with snow they are feasting on tropical insects. In the spring, they turn around and fly back north, but this time they fly over land.

Strong wings and stocky tail plumage help the blackpoll warbler to make its remarkable long-distance flight as shown on the map below.

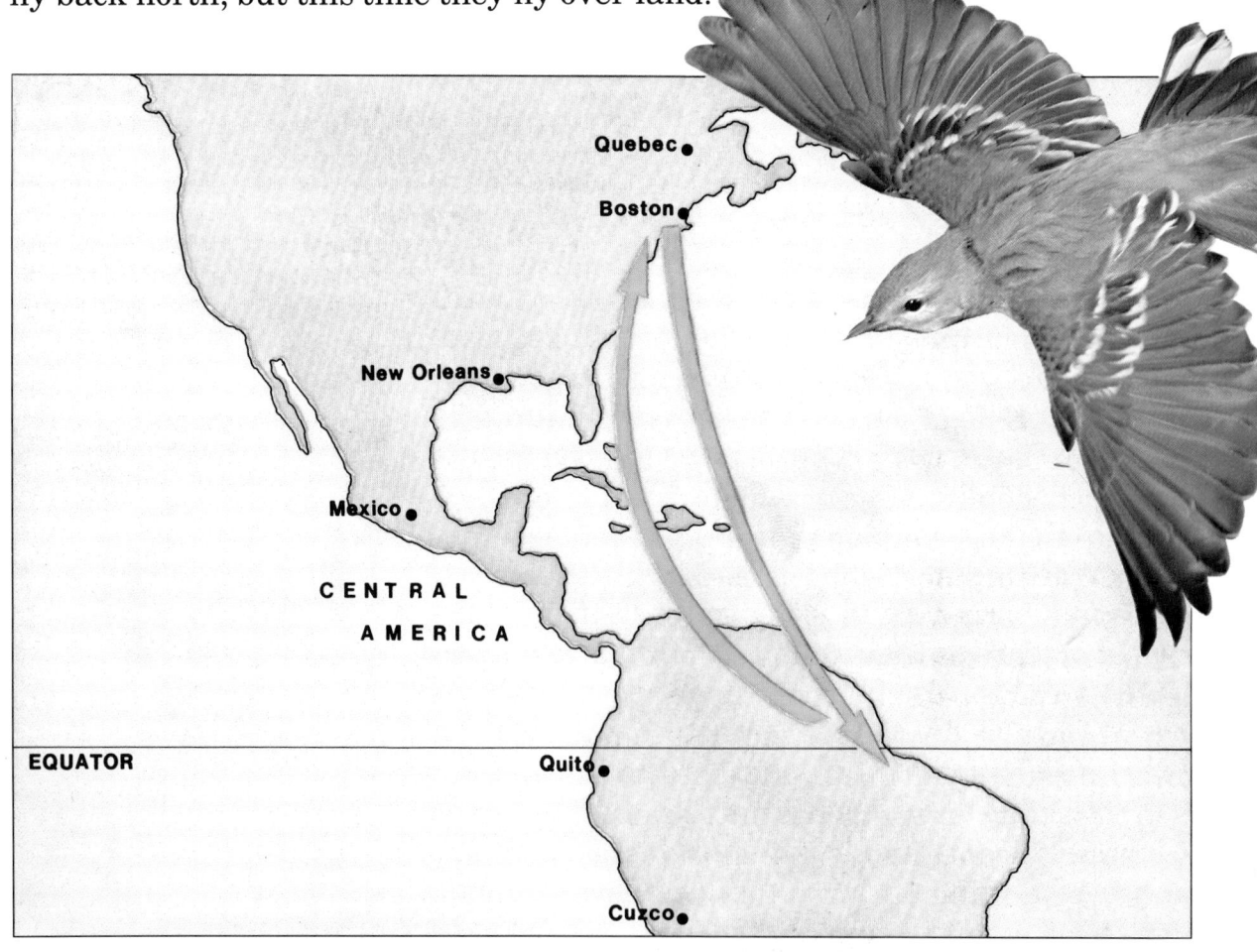

The 8,000 kilometre round-trip of the blackpoll warbler is just one example of the fantastic travels of many birds. Some fly huge distances: like the arctic tern voyaging 11,000 kilometres from Antarctica to the Arctic. Some are **precision** navigators. The Laysan albatross roams 130,000,000 square kilometres of the Pacific Ocean for two or three years, then finds its way home to Midway Island, its breeding ground, a mere five square kilometres.

A young Laysan albatross landing at Midway island in the Pacific ocean. When fully grown this bird will have a wing span of more than two metres. This is small compared with the wandering albatross which has a wing span of almost four metres.

## How do birds navigate?

It all seems very mysterious, birds being able to find their way around so accurately without any visible map or compass. What is the map that tells them where they are? Have they got a compass to steer them in the right direction? Scientists have watched thousands of birds of many different species to find out, but the answers are confusing.

Birds that migrate at night, like the European robin, can navigate by the stars. But instead of using a single star, like the Pole Star in the northern hemisphere, to guide them, they use the whole pattern of stars around the Pole. And if you raise young robins in a planetarium, you can teach them to use any set of stars as their compass. Robins, and many other birds, can also find their way when the sky is overcast, using a built-in magnetic compass.

For a scientist, the problem is that most birds migrate only twice a year. That makes it harder to study them. So scientists have turned to a bird that navigates to order.

## Homing pigeons

Homing pigeons are quite extraordinary navigators. They are taken from their home loft, put into a basket, and moved hundreds of kilometres away. When the baskets are opened, the pigeons rush out and head for home. No wonder biologists have tried to solve the mysteries of migration by studying homing pigeons.

Scientists have found out that these birds have many ways of finding their way home. If they are only a few kilometres from home, they simply check the landmarks, which they learn on training flights, to find their way. Further from home they have to use their built-in navigation instruments to provide a map and compass: they prefer to use the sun.

The sun rises in the east, swings overhead, and sets in the west. So it should be easy to use it as a guide, but since it moves across the sky there is a complication. They need to know the time of day. Say the bird wants to fly east. In the morning, that means flying towards the sun; but in the afternoon it means flying away from the sun.

A pigeon fancier with his racing pigeon. Pigeon racing is a sport carried out in many countries. The sport was developed in the 1840s, soon after pigeons were replaced as message carriers by the telegraph. Races are timed over various distances, sometimes as much as 1,000 kilometres.

A group of white pigeons at the entrance to their loft.

The picture shows a transporter from which racing pigeons are about to be released. This popular sport is based upon the ability of pigeons to find their way to the loft which is their home.

Pigeons tell the time of day from the pattern of darkness and light. Scientists in Europe proved this by tricking them. They took some pigeons to a loft north of their home. Then they kept the birds in the dark from midnight till noon, and turned on the lights from noon till midnight. So when it was actually noon, the birds thought it was dawn. To get home the birds would normally fly south. Because they thought it was dawn they set off with the sun on their left which would have taken them south if it had been dawn. In fact, as it was noon, the sun was in the south and if the birds had known this they would have flown towards the sun. In the end, they realized their 'mistake' and got home safely.

Pigeons have other instruments besides the sun. When the sky is overcast and the sun invisible they use their magnetic sense. In an experiment birds with a tiny magnet on their heads got lost, but those carrying a brass strip, which weighed the same but was not magnetic, found their way home. They can also smell their way and they can hear very low sounds, such as the crashing of waves on a beach, which can help them navigate. In another experiment birds that could not see properly, because they had been fitted with special contact lenses, set off in the right direction when they were released and landed near their loft, even if they did not get all the way back.

## Learning and instinct

Nobody knows how birds learn to find their way using the sun or stars; nor do we know how their magnetic sense works. But at least we know roughly what the birds are doing.

There is another puzzle about birds that migrate from their breeding grounds. How do the young birds, who have never made the journey, know where to go to find the wintering areas? Some, like the Bewick's swans that fly from Siberia to England, travel with their parents and obviously learn the route from them, but others, such as cuckoos, never see their parents, as they are raised by foster parents. Yet they still manage to find their way from Europe to Africa, so they must have an instinctive sense of direction. Many birds, however, combine learning and instinct.

Wildfowl feeding at the Wildfowl Trust, Welney, England. The birds in the foreground are Bewick's swans. These birds come from the tundras in northern Russia. In October, they migrate to warmer lands, such as England and northern Europe.

Some starlings are migratory. Here they are seen assembling on an English building before flying off to roost. Notice how evenly the birds have spaced themselves on the roof. They know just how far apart they need to perch so that wings do not clash when the birds fly off together.

Some starlings, for example, nest in countries near the Baltic Sea and spend the winter in England. In the autumn they fly first to Holland, and then across the North Sea to England. A Dutch scientist caught some starlings, put rings on them and took them to Switzerland. First he released the young birds and noted where they went. When they had vanished, he released the adults. That way, the young birds would not be able to follow the adults.

The adults ended up in northern France and some even made it to England. They had navigated properly, changing their course to end up in the right place even though the scientist had moved them. But the young birds turned up in the south of France and in Spain. They had simply flown on in the same direction in which they were heading before. This shows that these birds have an in-built sense of the direction in which they should go. Later they can learn to change their direction so as to reach a particular place.

A barnacle goose newly arrived at its tundra breeding ground in northern Canada. These birds are called barnacle geese because people in ancient times believed that they hatched out from barnacles in the sea!

When a female worker bee, called a scout, flies out in search of food she will probably meander along, twisting and turning. But having found the food, she makes a beeline straight back to the hive. That proves that she knows exactly where it is. Like the homing pigeon, she uses the sun as a compass.

## Using the sun

A simple experiment proves that bees can do this. You set out sugar water due east of the hive, and train the bees to feed there. Then you shut them in their hive for a few days. Just as with the pigeons, you change the pattern of light and darkness to fool the bees into thinking that it is dawn when it is really noon.

Now, you let them out of the hive to feed at noon. They think it is dawn, and fly straight towards the sun, as if the sun were due east, where they have learned the food is. But the sun is not east, it is south (in the northern hemisphere). So the bees end up in the wrong place, but only because you have interfered with their navigation system.

The head of a worker honeybee greatly magnified. The antennae are each divided into segments and provide the bee with her senses of smell and touch. The bee has two very large compound eyes on either side of the head. There are also small simple eyes, one of which you can see at the top of the forehead. These are some of the devices that enable bees to navigate so well.

Two worker honeybees approaching a flower in their search for nectar. Look at the bee on the right of the picture. The antennae are pointing towards the flower. One large compound eye is clearly visible. You can also see the pollen basket on the rear leg.

The sun, of course, is not always visible. Bees can still navigate because they can detect other clues. They can see **polarized** light, which makes the sky look very different.

Some areas of sky look darker than others. The bees can use the different sky patterns to find their way. They can also detect the Earth's magnetic field, using a small compass needle in their head.

## How bees give directions

When a scout gets back to her hive, she dances on the honeycomb to tell her sisters where the food is. She runs along the comb, waggling from side to side. Then she loops back and does the waggling run again. The workers, who follow the dance, soon set off in search of the food, and they find it so quickly that they must have been given directions. But how?

Worker bees at the entrance to their hive. They come and go busily in their hunt for pollen and nectar. One of their duties is to fan their wings near the hive entrance in order to keep the hive cool.

## The dance of the bees

Karl von Frisch, an Austrian scientist, discovered how the dance tells the bees where to go. Von Frisch marked each bee who arrived at a feeding station with a spot of paint. Back at the hive he watched the marked bee dance. After painstaking work, involving many experiments over several years, he decoded the language of the dance.

The angle of the waggling run tells the workers in which direction to go. If the run is straight up the comb, that means: fly towards the sun. If it is straight down: fly away from it. And if the bee runs horizontally across the comb, that means fly at right angles to the direction of the sun.

The speed of the dance tells the workers how far to fly. A slow dance, with many waggles, means the food is far away. A fast dance, with fewer waggles, means it is close by. And the smell of the flower, which the scout passes to the workers in a drop of nectar, tells them what sort of scent to look out for.

Returning from a collecting trip, worker bees do a nectar dance on the honeycomb. Any bee that has information about new food sources can indicate the direction, the distance and even the size of the find by means of this dance.

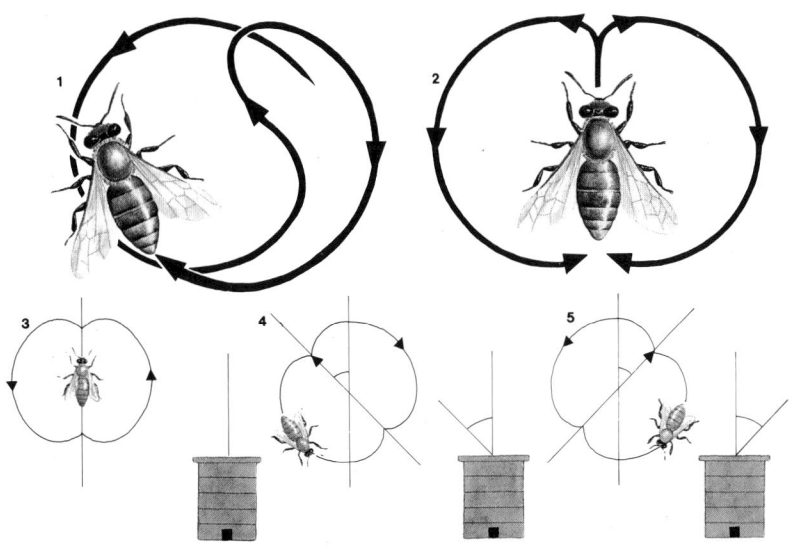

1. When the food source is close to the hive, the scout performs a round dance.
2. When the food is far away, she dances in the form of a figure eight. The speed of the dance indicates the distance of the food.
3, 4, 5. The scout points in a definite direction from the hive, while waggling her abdomen. The angle is related to the position of the sun. The other bees navigate by using the sun as a marker.

## How did the code come into being?

This system enables bees to be very efficient. Each morning, scouts fan out across the countryside, looking for new patches of flowers that have come into bloom. They keep track of where they are by looking at the sun, or by the pattern of polarization in the sky. When they find food, they make a beeline back to the hive to get a team of new workers to gather the food while it is available. The scouts use the waggle dance to tell the workers where to go and what to look for.

Nobody knows exactly how this system started. Perhaps, to begin with, a scout might actually have taken the workers to the food. She would come back to the hive, get others excited about her find, and lead them to the flowers. Perhaps some scouts turned back to gather more recruits. Their direction of take-off would point at the food. Eventually, they might only pretend to take off. This could be the origin of the waggling run. Other bees would follow the run and work out the direction to go.

The most difficult thing to explain is the change, from dancing outside the hive and dancing inside. We really have no good idea how this happened. But it certainly works, and a dancing robot bee, operated by a computer, will send bees exactly where the programmer tells it.

# 4 Navigating in the Air: Butterflies and Bats

It is not only birds that travel through the air. Baby spiders drift off on parachutes of silk. Grasshoppers swarm in search of food. Some butterflies travel long distances in search of shelter.

The most famous of these is the monarch butterfly, which lives in America. In the autumn, monarchs in the north begin to fly south in large swarms. Many successfully travel between 2,000 and 3,000 kilometres to reach their destinations in Texas, California and Mexico. There, they hang on trees in huge numbers, conserving their energy until spring, when they start heading north again, laying eggs as they go.

Butterflies, including the monarch, use the sun to find their way, but unlike birds and bees they do not have an in-built clock to adjust for the sun's movement. So the track of a migrating butterfly is a series of loops, each loop equal to one day. In the morning, they travel too far to the east, and in the afternoon too far to the west; over several days the loops cancel out, so they travel in one direction.

A huge mass of monarch butterflies mill around as they reach their winter quarters in Mexico. These famous migrants will settle on selected trees as shown above, and will stay there during the winter months. When the spring comes they will fly back north again in a mass.

Fruit bats in northern Queensland, Australia. During the hours of daylight, these bats hang from trees in large clusters. At night they visit fruit trees in swarms, sometimes flying as much as fifty kilometres to get food.

The black flying fox, here seen hanging on a banana tree, is the largest of the Australian fruit bats. These animals are found in tropical Australia and in Papua New Guinea.

## Migrating bats

Bats are another great group of flying migrants. Many make special journeys from the roost they use in summer to a different place more suitable for hibernating in winter. In Britain the journeys are short, not much more than 20 kilometres. But in North America, Indiana bats spend the winter in caves in Kentucky and then fly 500 kilometres north for the summer. Some Russian pipistrelle bats travel more than 1,000 kilometres to hibernate.

In Australia and the Pacific, the large fruit bats (also called flying foxes), fly off each day as dusk falls, to trees that have ripe fruit. The distance may be 20 kilometres or more, and when one tree has no fruit left they must find another that does. On these journeys the fruit bats probably find their way about because they know the area around their roost. Some species of fruit bat, like the Australian flying fox, also make long migrations each year to places that are good for breeding.

# 5 | Navigating on Land

Theseus was a Greek hero, who went to slay the Minotaur, a monster who lived in the middle of a complicated maze. Everyone who had previously tried to kill the Minotaur had got lost in the labyrinth but a woman called Ariadne gave Theseus a silken thread. He tied one end of it to the entrance of the maze, and followed the thread to find his way out when he had killed the Minotaur.

Limpets are great navigators! You can read about them in the text on this page. This photograph shows a group of limpets marked with paint for a homing experiment. These limpets wandered about freely at high tide and then each one returned to the exact spot as the tide receded.

Some spiders do exactly the same. Whenever they leave the safety of their hiding place they attach a silk thread. When danger threatens they drop to the ground, climbing back along the thread to safety when all is clear.

Limpets, the flattened snails that live on rocks by the seaside, do the same sort of thing. At high tide the limpet wanders about, grazing on the **algae** that grow on the rock, but it always returns to the same spot before the tide goes out. This is where the limpet's shell fits the rock particularly closely; and to be able to find it again the limpet **secretes** a chemical trail that somehow points the way back home. Each limpet follows only its own trail. If you scrub the rock clean while the limpets are feeding, they all become lost.

# Ant navigators

Ants lay trails too, droplets that guide their nest-mates to food and help them all get back home. Some trails seem to contain signposts that tell the ant which way to go. If you persuade some ants to travel along a twig, and then you turn the twig around, they may become confused because the sun gives them one message and the trail says the opposite.

Following a trail is not really navigation, because without the trail the animal is quite literally lost. But ants are also capable of real navigation. Some do it by remembering the pattern of plants silhouetted against the sky during the journey. Others use polarized light, like bees. And some use the sun as a compass. A mirror placed carefully next to a line of ants may make them all turn round and start heading in the opposite direction.

A harvester ants' nest in West Africa, showing trails.

A herd of caribou seen migrating in northern Canada.

# The migrating herds

One of the most dramatic migrations on land is the annual journey of the herds that live in the Serengeti in East Africa. In December, at the end of the dry season, vast herds of wildebeeste, Thomson's gazelles, and zebras move out of the scrubby woodlands around the edge of Lake Victoria and on to the grassy plain of the Serengeti. They go wherever rain is falling, because the rain makes the grass grow and will provide good food. The herds seem to move towards storm clouds and thunder, even when these are 100 kilometres away.

The general pattern is to follow the rain in an anti-clockwise direction although the exact route varies from year to year. By June, when the rains stop, the herds are moving back to the woodlands, which are wetter and so provide food even when the plains are dry and dusty.

Hyenas may follow the herds and prey on the weakest, but other animals in the Serengeti do not migrate. Lions, for example, stay in one area and feed on the wildebeeste only when they come through it. Giraffes and impala do not migrate either. But they have their young when the great migration is passing through. So many animals are passing through that there is less chance of a young impala or giraffe falling prey to **predators**.

Opposite: Seen from the air, the migration of wildebeeste is like a trail of harvester ants (see the picture on page 23). These large animals are not stopped by the Mara river. They plunge across, swimming if they need to, to keep up with the others. A strange thing is the way they line up for the crossing like a troop of soldiers.

Above: Wildebeeste and zebra crossing the Mara river on their migration.

Left: A hot air balloon over Kenya. In the foreground, a herd of zebra move over the grassy savannah as they migrate. The zebra's main enemy is the lion.

# 6 Navigating under Water

Travelling through water is difficult because it may be hard to see the sun or stars and currents can sweep the animal off course. Despite that, many creatures do make long and accurate journeys through the water.

Spiny lobsters spend the summer on the coral reefs of the Caribbean. As winter approaches, they start to head for deep water. They form a queue, each lobster touching the one in front, and begin to walk deeper and deeper. That takes them below the damage caused by winter storms, and perhaps also away from predators. It may also help save food because deep water is cold and when they are cold the lobsters need less energy and so need less to eat.

Spiny lobsters are found around California and in the Caribbean. These five lobsters keep close together as they 'march' towards deeper, safer waters.

Fish migrate too. Some simply swim from the reef where they live, to nearby mangrove swamps to spawn. Others go on long circular journeys. Some cod travel from Iceland to Greenland and back again. Herrings journey round the North Sea. And of course the fishermen follow them. But perhaps the most famous migrating fish is the salmon.

A salmon ladder near Loch More, Caithness, Scotland. This helps the migrating salmon to climb up towards their breeding grounds.

Leaping salmon use their strength to climb the rapids in a Scottish river.

## From ocean to river

Salmon breed in shallow streams. The **fry** move downstream and enter the sea. They swim off from many streams, joining others and ending up in large shoals. After several years' feeding at sea, the adult salmon return to breed in the very same stream where they were born. That ought to be a good place to breed, because they were born there and survived.

Nobody is exactly sure how the salmon find their way from the open ocean to the coast where their river enters the sea. Once there, they may smell or taste their way home, following chemicals that give each stream its distinct character. The urge to swim upstream is strong; salmon spend great energy leaping up falls and rapids. Where people build dams or weirs, they should add a salmon ladder, that enables the fish to continue their journey upstream.

## From river to ocean

Eels make the reverse journey; they spawn in the sea and the adults live in fresh water. European and North American eels lay their eggs in the Sargasso Sea in the Atlantic. The fry drift with the currents until they get close to land. Then they change into **elvers**, which swim up rivers and become adults. The adults feed and, when they are mature, return to the Sargasso Sea to breed. Their journey remains a mystery because no adult eels have ever been caught far from land.

## The biggest navigators

Whales, the biggest creatures in the world, make long migrations. Many species of whale feed during the summer in icy polar waters, then migrate to regions closer to the Equator to give birth in the winter. Grey whales swim from Alaska past California to Mexico. If they delay, they may get trapped in the ice.

Elvers (young eels) migrating upstream in Britain.

Grey whales trapped in ice at Barrow, in Alaska, October 1988. They were eventually rescued by animal lovers.

# 7 | People and Navigation

Some scientists say that people, like pigeons, whales, and bees, have an in-built compass. In some experiments, people wearing magnets on their heads were not so good at pointing the direction home as people without. Other scientists tried to repeat this experiment but could not. They say we have no in-built compass and the argument goes on. I do not know who is correct, but I do know that even without that kind of compass, people can be every bit as good as the most skilled animal navigators at finding their way about.

All over the world, there are still people who can find the way without written maps. The Australian Aborigines are famous for their journeys. They still have the skills handed down from their ancestors. They may go wandering through the bush, often with a more experienced guide. They teach the young ones the routes and the secrets of survival by building a map in their minds. They use so many different clues to tell them where they are that it would be impossible to list them all: sun, stars, colour of rock, position of clouds, types of plants, animal tracks, river-beds and even termite mounds.

The first people to live in Australia were the Aborigines. They knew how to find their way around, and to survive like the old man in the picture. They knew about plants and animals, and where to find water. They were never lost.

The most famous navigators, however, are the people of the South Seas. They used to make long journeys in small boats across the vast Pacific Ocean. Often their target was a tiny island that would be easy to miss, but they almost always found it.

The navigator was a very important and respected person in the community. He spent a long apprenticeship, sailing with an expert. He learned the star constellations that indicated the direction of different island groups. He would lie on his back in the bottom of the boat, feeling the pattern of waves in different parts of the ocean. He learned to see differences in the colour of the water beneath the boat, in the behaviour of the fishes and birds, and in the position of clouds. Important routes had a song, which the navigator memorized. The words of the song contained instructions for the journey.

Eventually the young navigator was ready to guide his own crew on these immense journeys across thousands of kilometres of water. With such skills, the ancient Polynesians covered a huge area, from Hawaii in the north to Easter Island in the south-east and New Zealand in the south-west. The old ways were dying out but now young people are again taking pride in the skills of their ancestors and there are races around the Pacific to see who is the best navigator.

Outrigger sailing taking place near the Caroline islands in the southern Pacific ocean. Though these are young enthusiasts of the present day, they use the same skills and the same kind of boats that their ancestors used.

# Astounding Facts

- An arctic tern ringed in Wales turned up in New South Wales, in Australia, six months later. That is a journey of at least 20,000 kilometres.

- The dwarf bee dances outdoors, and indicates the direction by raising her **abdomen** like a flag.

- A herd of bison migrating across the Arkansas River in 1871 was 80 kilometres long and 25 kilometres wide.

- Not all birds migrate by flying. Little auks swim hundreds of kilometres from the Arctic to spend the winter off the coast of Newfoundland. And Emperor penguins swim and walk 500 to 600 kilometres through the ice to reach their rookeries.

- Pink salmon migrate up to 4,000 kilometres from the stream where they were born, but return there to lay their eggs.

- Cars often squash frogs and toads migrating across roads to breed in ponds, and the animals can be a hazard to traffic. In some places, tunnels under the road save the animals and the drivers.

- When whales get lost, they often end up stranded on a beach. Strandings happen most often after magnetic storms, which might upset the whales' compass.

- Green turtles swim 3,000 kilometres from Brazil to Ascension Island, navigating by sun and stars.

# Glossary

**abdomen**: the hind part of an insect's body. In mammals, the abdomen is the belly.

**algae**: very simple plants that do not have proper roots, stems or leaves. They are found in damp places and in water.

**aluminium**: a silvery-white metal that is light and does not rust.

**elver**: a young eel.

**fry**: young fish.

**hibernate**: to pass the cold winter months, when food is scarce, in a sleeping (dormant) and inactive state.

**polarized**: describes light that moves in one direction, rather than in every direction.

**precision**: accuracy and exactness.

**predator**: any animal that hunts and eats other animals. Lions are predators.

**radar**: a system of bouncing radio waves off objects to detect them, and to work out how far they are away.

**secrete**: to make and give out a substance that is produced by a gland in animals or plants.

**species**: a class of animals or plants that look alike. Members of one species cannot usually breed with those of another species.

**tundra**: cold, treeless plains of the Arctic regions.

# Index

You can use this index for looking up different animals, and the parts of the world where some of them are found. Where a page number is printed in *italic* (slanting) type, it means that there is a picture of that animal on that page, as well as text.

Africa 4, 14
Alaska 4, 5, 28
albatross 9, *11*
algae 22
ant *23*
Antarctica 3, 11
Arkansas River 31
Arctic 3, 4, 11, 31
arctic tern *3*, 11, 31
Ascension Island 31
Atlantic 10, 28
Australia 6, 8, 21, 29, 31
Austria 18

bald eagle *4*, 5
Baltic Sea 15
barnacle goose *15*
Barrow 28
bat *21*
bee *16*, *17*, *18*, *19*, 23, 29
Bermuda 10
Bewick's swan *14*
bison 31
black flying fox *21*
blackpoll warbler *10*, 11
Brazil 10, 31
Britain 8, 21, 28
brown bear *5*

Caithness 27
California 9, 20, 26, 28
Canada 10, 15, 23
Canada goose *3*, *9*
Caribbean 10, 26

caribou 4, *23*
Caroline Islands 30
Central America 6
cod 26
condor 9
crocodile *8*
cuckoo 14

Denmark 7
dwarf bee 31

East Africa 24
Easter Island 30
eel *28*
elver *28*
Emperor penguin 31
England 14, 15
Europe 4, 5, 6, 11, 14, 28

flying fox *21*
France 7, 15
frog 31
fruit bat *21*

gharial *8*
giraffe 24
grasshopper 20
Greenland 26
green turtle 31
grey whale *28*

harvester ant *23*, 24
Hawaii 30
herring 26
Holland 15

homing pigeon *12*, *13*, 16
honeybee *16*, *17*, *18*, *19*
hyena 24

Iceland 26
impala 24
Indiana bat 21
Israel 6, 7

Kentucky 21
Kenya 24

Lake Victoria 24
Laysan albatross *11*
limpet *3*, *22*
lion 24
little auk 31
lobster *26*

Mara River 24, 25
Mexico 20, 28
Midway Island 11
monarch butterfly *20*

Nepal 8
New England 10
New South Wales 31
New Zealand 30
Newfoundland 31
North Africa 6
North America 4, 5, 21, 28

Pacific Ocean 11, 21, 30
Papua New Guinea 21

pelican 6
pigeon *12*, *13*, 16, 29
pink salmon 31
pipistrelle bat 21

Queensland 21

robin 11
Russia 14, 21

salmon *4*, *5*, 26, *27*
Sargasso Sea 28
Scotland 27
seal 9
Serengeti 24
Siberia 14
snow goose *3*
South America 4, 8
South Seas 30
Spain 15
spider 20, 22
spiny lobster *26*
starling *15*
swallow 4, *6*, 7
Switzerland 15

termite 29
Texas 20
Thomson's gazelle 24
toad 31

USA 4, 5, 10
USSR 8

Wales 31
wandering albatross 11
water vole 4
West Africa 23
whale 9, *28*, 29, 31
white pelican *6*
wildebeeste *24*, *25*

zebra *24*

# Further Reading and Study

If you have enjoyed reading this book and want to learn more about animals and how they behave, there are several things you can do:

- You can read the other five titles in this series. They are listed on the back cover. This will widen your knowledge of animal behaviour.

- Learn all you can about the animals that interest you most. Look them up in a natural history encyclopedia or other reference book.

- Learn about other series of books dealing with wildlife, for example:
  Discovering Nature series published by Wayland
  Eyewitness Guides published by Dorling Kindersley, and by Collins in Australia
  Mysteries and Marvels of Nature published by Usborne
  Today's World published by Watts/Gloucester

- If you have a pet, increase your knowledge of animal behaviour by watching how your pet behaves.

# Picture Acknowledgements

The publishers wish to thank the following photographers and agencies whose photographs appear in this book. The photographs are credited below by page number and position on the page, B bottom, T top:

Ardea London Ltd: Jack Bailey 7B, Dr C. H. McDougal, 8, A. Greensmith 9T, S. Roberts 9B, John Mason 17B, Jean-Paul Ferrero 21T, Hans and Judy Beste 21B, François Gohier 28B; Bruce Coleman Ltd: Gordon Langsbury 3T, 14, Jeff Foott 4T, 7T, Jane Burton 6B, 28T, Francis Lanting 11, Kim Taylor 17T, Peter Ward 23T, Peter Davey 24B, J. Pearson 25, Robert Schroeder 26, Nicholas Devore 30; Eric and David Hosking: 3B, 10T, 15T; Frank Lane Picture Agency: W. Wisniewski 5, W. Broadhurst 12, Treat Davidson 18, Ron Austing 20T, Frank Lane 20B, 24T, R. Thompson 27B; Nature Photographers Ltd: Hugh Miles 4B, 15B, 23B, M. Muller & H. Wohlmuth 6T, N. A. Callow 16, Andrew Cleave 22, Paul Sterry 27T; ZEFA: 13T, 13B, 29.